CW00531028

Sabine Wichert was born in Graudenz, West Prussia (now Grudziadz, Poland) in 1942 and grew up in West Germany. Educated at various German and English universities, she has taught history at Queen's University, Belfast, since 1971. She has published two previous collections of poetry: *Tin Drum Country* (Salmon Publishing, 1995) and *Sharing Darwin* (Salmon Publishing, 1999).

By the same author

Poetry
Tin Drum Country
Sharing Darwin

History
Northern Ireland Since 1945

As Editor
Chattel, Servant or Citizen:
Women's Status in Church, State and Society
(co-edited with Mary O'Dowd)

From the United Irishmen to Twentieth-Century Unionism:
A Festschrift for A.T.Q. Stewart

TAGANROG

TAGANROG

SABINE WICHERT

LAGAN PRESS
BELFAST
2004

Acknowledgements

The publishers would like to acknowledge the editors of the following magazines in which some of the following poems first appeared: *Envoi, Fortnight, HU, Orbis, Poetry Nottingham International, Windows* and *Writing Women.*   .

Some of these poems were written in Anne O'Dowd's house in Co. Sligo and many in the Tyrone Guthrie Centre at Annamakerrig. The author is very grateful to both.

Published by
Lagan Press
Unit 11
1A Bryson Street
Belfast BT5 4ES
e-mail: lagan-press@e-books.org.uk
web: lagan-press.org.uk

ARTS
COUNCIL
of Northern Ireland

ISBN: 1 904652 12 3
Author: Wichert, Sabine
Title: Taganrog
2004

Set in Sabon
Printed by Easyprint, Belfast

Contents

Early September, Unromantic

The greens become uniform
as they gently slide towards colour—
no longer the twenty-five different
shades of early summer.

The young bull wearing sunglasses
over just one eye, pees, eats and
rubs his flank against the tree all
in one move. Strange, how for once

I can see only walking beef
in the countryside: these bulls seem
on the edge of fighting half
the time, else eat and defecate,

as if nature with the first taste
of autumn in the air offered
nothing but harvests and dinners
for all its kinds.

Past and Presence

In the past they took an eye for an eye,
they worshipped the golden calves and practised
nepotism. They put people to the stake
in the past and enjoyed watching them burn.

Is the past ever past?—In your spare time,
you used to say, when you did not investigate
the past, you thought of me. Perhaps, I thought,
when driving to an unimportant lunch appointment,

or when the children's peas had to be divided
evenly between their plates. Those children
are older now: their sense of fair play has
widened or deepened or disappeared.

Now, if they can, they take two eyes for one;
the calves have grown into fit and healthy
bulls and most of the burning is done in private
or covered up, the tortured kept silent.

The Real Tree
for Grainne

She wants to paint the tree
until the bark flies;
she draws its leaves,
assaults its shoots and suckers,
batters its trunk
with her charcoal,
thrusts her pencil
at limb and branch,
drives her brush
against bough and twig
until it's winter-bare.

She follows its lines
gently down to the branching,
the spreading and dividing,
coaching it, come
what may,
into the picture;
goes down to its roots
lovingly, softly
unfolds its cells
where surely
life must flow.

She wants the real tree
on her canvas,
the reality of the tree.
And the tree sways for her,
unfolds for her:
leaves turning in the wind,
twigs and branches,
bark and stem,
roots, cells even;
but its reality
evades her.

Getting into the Mood

I stare out of my window
at 'Please Use the Car Park'
and wait for inspiration.

No time for a drink until
later; I ration myself
to wait for revelations.

A lawn behind the sign, a field,
bushes, a tree, and the swans
with their cygnets glide on the lake.

More trees and fields beyond.
Is that enough for creativity
to spring its unexpected source?

No oblivion in company,
but watching the birds, the cows
and the man mowing the lawn.

Be alert, alert for intuitions,
watch the other artists talk
to themselves and the man on the lawn.

I stare at the sign and suddenly
know what is wrong with this landscape:
too many words and too much green.

Mismatched

Yours was a tidy garden
where roses followed bluebells
followed tulips followed
snowdrops, moving safely
onto dahlias and asters;
and as you sat among your
flowers behind hedges, you
often wished a jungle would
follow you into the house,
creep up the stairs and envelop
you in its lushness.

When I showed you the jungle
that is my garden, where few
rules apply and little can
be predicted, you stayed close
to the gate and asked for a
chair; even though my paths
were wildly overgrown and
difficult to fathom, you did
not want to be engulfed
and thus we never visited
each other's fantasies.

Irish July

I didn't believe it would turn warm.
Now I'm sweating in all my sweaters,
when the skin cries out for the sun.

Northern August

Lulled into flaccidity
by days and days of warmth
when even the sunshine
no longer warrants a comment,
we hardly notice
that slyly the tension
begins to build again:
what will autumn withhold
and winter threaten?

Waiting at Honeysuckle Cottage

Every time I pass 'Honeysuckle Cottage'
she sits on the wooden bench by her front door
which is unadorned by any flowers. She
does not look old, but has not been young for some
time. She seems to wait. Her hands lie unfolded

in her lap: they sometimes hold a book or stroke
the wood or the material of her skirt
as she lifts her face to passers-by. Mostly
her eyes are on the ground in front of her, on
the brown-sandy soil between patches of grass

and weeds as if she expected something more
substantial to grow there any time now. I
hardly have time to stop: her patience is
the other side of my hurry, my tomorrow
is her time—only time, which does not need haste

to be caught. Once the cancer has started you
hope for a future, but wait for death, or a
god to rescue you, as you waited for love
and then thought it had come, and then waited again.
One day she lifted her head and smiled at me.

Ventures

People might recognise and shatter me
during their morning outings. When they
stop to greet me or chat, or even just
smile at me in the shops, or the neighbour
gives me a friendly nod, I am chilled
by their evil conspiracy with the weather.

Sometimes, though, the street holds the
sky a little higher, tentatively I step
on to the black ice and find that
I can control some of my steps
and walking becomes easier

than for a long time: I do not always
need to hold on to fences or to look
away for fear that a friendly smile
might smash me. Something is beginning
to hold together again; if I am careful
I may venture out now and then.

The Yellow Devil

The yellow one, the ancient one is back
and makes my juices rise, my bile hiccup,
the blood-poisoner, the evil-eyed devil
got me again. I shall send you a Valentine:
race through

my heart, fall back on romance. I'll draw
secret ink from him, open my veins, wet
my dreams, let you draw from where you
are not to be. Yet the wobble-kneed one
bites and

hurts: that shaky-fingered faint-heart,
the evil sorcerer, all guilt-familiar,
and always virtuously to be obeyed. They
tell me he is green here: is all the island
jealous, then?

Incongruous

A foolish Dutchman talking
about an overrated
Irish poet to a
Japanese audience
which had difficulties
with his accent.

Decision

She cannot face losing her hair as well;
her body was so beautiful before
this mutilation, she'd rather die—
until she realises that women do.

The Smell of Frying Cheese

Sometimes she woke to the noise of soldiers
and the alien smell of frying cheese.
They'd bivouac under the ancient trees
by the side of the dirt-road. Those oaks
almost saw Napoleon, it was said,
but he didn't quite make it this way. The war
was over, but the locals remained

suspicious. They did not like this freedom—
bringing British soldiers with their gibberish
and gypsies' ways. You could not trust what was
not yours. She, too, had learned to be cautious,
curious, careful, alert and ready
to run as she had had to with her parents

from faraway places bowing to
the patterns of centuries: if you can,
move on. The natives had stayed put, kept their
heads down and survived. By now the soldiers
paid for their eggs, chicken and milk; they had

brought freedom, they said, but no food. Neither
were heroes or rebels watching each other
with beady eyes. By then she had also learnt
to respect but never trust uniforms.

She left before she was quite one of them
and often thought of ancient oaks, the smell
of frying cheese, the need to survive and move on.

Through the Window

A bit heavy on the adjectives, he'd said, if
you are clever, don't show it: writing in the pool
of her own warm appreciation she felt
it less hot than it used to be.

A face at the window, others passing by.
—Is this where the artists are, then?
—I can't really say, said the man
edging the lawn.

She looks out at them looking in at her,
or at the window behind which they
think her; while their boys climb
into the treehouse, they photograph
the lake and wander off. Suddenly
they shout back for the children, long
and loud, and finally succeed in
cutting the thread of her thought.

Shake the words until they fit,
smooth them into the fabric,
use edgy ones for the corners,
let them expand for gothic effect;
if they don't fit, store them,
if they won't obey, throw them out;
let them breathe gently through strong structures
or cough ecstatically for a thunderstorm;
go easy on the adjectives.

Laying Poison

The old, unevenly lettered, hand-painted rusty
board, POISON LAYED, at the gate to the field has
been replaced by a shiny new plastic and professionally
printed one: Beware of Cross Fresian Bull. Enter
at your own risk.

After your visit to the golden wedding in Strabane,
where unemployment pushes against and meets
the border, your watercolours dissolved into reality.

More deadly, civilisations without wars?
The indeterminable breakdown. But of what?

Sitting around the master table somewhere: strategy
and tactics: how to employ their forces, which hills
to take, which villages to clear, how many buildings
to eliminate and which people to cleanse.

Mapping death and destruction:
why maps were invented, what we are about.

Snow

This was not the promised
end of our beginning:
there was no snow that year,
the earth stayed open and   .
vulnerable; birds fed
all winter; the grey skies
emptied themselves only
of rain. Cold fog lay long
in the valleys; it was
the beginning of our end.

The Affair

Happy memories
and flirty allusions
hit her ear;
she puts the phone
down crying.

They loved each other
for a week or two,
but he remembers
the happy days
and she their ending.

Moonwanderer

Children playing at darkening corners,
stray dogs half-busy and alert; my lips
defiant against the gaining moon, my
stride not slowing as if these streets were

unfamiliar. This afternoon's friendship was
too easy and too open, now the wind is wet
and vicious, biting into my eyes. How strange
these walks, how outcast these pavements

make me feel, if only because I'm
no longer fearful, no longer cold, yet
look longingly at the imagined warmth
of all these houses: if only because at

last I want to go back to wherever I came
from, whatever that now may be—my father's
land? my mother's land? my land? land
of illusion, refuge of the imagination, dreamland:

home is where you make it. The dogs are
fighting, the children should be home by
now, sadness in every bone I slow and
brave the greying moon, the open streets.

Envy

After two husbands, four children, and six books
she can afford to gather her friends comfortably:
the coffee pot is ready, the bottle handy, the typewriter
stands sentry on the sideboard. I try to be
brilliant, but that does not work, nor does my

boasting. The more I watch the more I feel
lost, the more I retreat into childhood. They
seem so locked in understanding and embracing
each other's lives, so far away; I dare not
touch their chairs or draw into their circle.

I listen but only half-comprehend what seems
complete and full of life outside my own,
envious, angry, sulkingly, wanting to imitate,
if clumsily. The days grow distant and my nights
can't cope with all the dreams that watching her induces.

Wavelengths

When she arrived he took her under his wings
where she nourished her language to flying point,
where they shared spaghetti and jazz, his family
and long walks in the dunes with the dog, birthday
parties and operas, where conversation seemed easy:
sentences, signals, jokes and references bounced like

balls between them as would simple banter and
the forgiving tease between siblings, and their fights
were just as quick: a flair, a jump, an insult thrown,
a flying return and then they'd laugh together at
the follies of the world—but then, one day the laughter
was empty, the hours dragged, the weather changed,

his wings appeared threadbare and thin; her grasp
of words and their meaning had outgrown his,
and once she could say what she had tried to say for
years, there was no longer meaning in their conversation:
it gaped open and bleak, their languages were
foreign to each other, they shared a world no longer.

Bells

A cat sat on the window sill
preening itself, and I felt as
contented, when the message
came by telephone: the hustle
is over, you are gone.
Even my tears felt cold.

You did not let the doctors
look until it was too late—
you never had the measure
of your own flesh: you
did not allow the bell to ring
and now it tolls for you.

October

Don't meet or mate, they say,
when the apples have ripened,
no new seed will germinate,
you've left it too late for nature.

But then, you can always defy
them: be human, have spring
or summer in autumn or
winter: no need to multiply.

Expatriate Visiting Home

His face looked different from various angles
as if he hadn't grown a final one and every
place he'd stayed had shaped and added to
it as he left some of his life behind.

He remembered little of Bangkok, or that's
what he let us believe, but there was a Bewley's
in Tokyo where the Irish met every day, and
he missed the wines of Paris wherever he now

went; he knew the opening hours in Tokyo
but could not help us with Monaghan's
pubs. He walked through the landscape
glumly as if he couldn't remember it all,

and day after day grew lively at opening
time, when wine and whiskey appeared. He
had left, he said, because people here
did not know how to enjoy themselves.

Dream

They'd put her into a coffin
shaped like a drawer of the chest
in which she kept her manuscripts
and letters, her diaries and typescripts;
she should have escaped while there
was time: now it was too late; but
she did not deserve this, she felt,
she had been bad, but not that bad.

They had taken her naked
out of her sheets and pressed
her into the drawer. Silently
she shouted: wait, wait, I need
to put on a gown, I'm not this naked...

When she woke up she could not remember
the end: there had been twisted complications
and she thought she hadn't quite died and
it had not quite been a nightmare. But as
she tried hard to recall, and she needed to
understand, all she remembered were the mummies
in large jars and the spirits about the house
she'd read about before she fell asleep.

The Painting

Your painting was pure innocence
when I first hung it on my wall,
catching the best light in the house.
Soft almost-white with those few
bright yellow and blue and very
precise lines. Then the colours
began to glow and slowly a rosy
hue obliterated the lines, intensifying
until I came down one day
to a house steeped in red:

dripped down from your painting,
trickled along the brown wall over
the red skirting-board, red as the
carpet, red into the blood-soaked
carpet. How did I let it happen?
How did I let the blood run, where
will it run now that it fills the house?

Vacation

Sweet sweat near the sea and
the smell of salty oysters: we
could not get enough of it
and every time it tasted better.

While I was hooked on misery,
looking across the seas to damp
loughs and forbidden meetings,
you thought of your allotment
and how in your absence
the marrows would ripen.

Easy to kindle fires on
Mediterranean shores, easy
to stoke them and love
their heat without regret.

After we said goodbye
at the Delphic oracle, with
a dried leaf to remember
and a last embrace, the
hot ashes lingered and
kept us warm for a while.

To a Student

In a well-tended garden everything appears to fit in
just so. Sometimes the garden will need digging, however
shy you are of fork and spade, if only to bury some
of the accumulated rubbish or to make room for
something new. Last night the rain washed the front
of this terrace of houses and soon it will do their
backs. Let go now and then, let things happen,
uncontrolled, and risk the detrimental: not
everything rejected makes good compost for you, but
it may come in handy to your neighbour cultivating his.

Don't worry; read your parents' horticultural books;
fathers have always known how to serve and command
you. You'll not be lost, as long as you trust them.
Don't trust them: your life is yours. Dig your own
soil and you'll know what it can hold, what it will
grow—such as your faith, if you really need
it. But the faithful too have their dumps: Golgotha
caused compost and rubbish in equal measure.
Watch that faith, any faith, or it will eat you as a
weed or a pest can slowly strangle your garden.

Coriander in the Rain

Shiny bright fruit growing high
on trees, always out of reach.
They hardly throw a shadow.

Your urge to devour the exotic:
green chillies, coriander and
turmeric; then later coconut,
pawpaw and guava, mango,
orange, kiwi and quinces.

What you cannot eat you try
to remember: magnolia,
orchids and bougainvillaea;
the exuberance of colours
defying imagination: jasmine,
amaryllis and granadilla.

For one day soon you'll have
to go home again to Sunday
roasts with two dull veg
and a summer pudding at best.
Do you hear the rain waiting for you?

Graz, August 1994

In the public garden in front
of the university a light
breeze makes roses and
lavender dance an unexpected
late summer duet.

People pass, talking,
reading, going somewhere;
my half-thoughts are on
a plane to Tel Aviv
as I laze in the sun.

As I move through the day,
I note the timbre of people's
voices, their gracious
movements and how
often they smile.

How often can one repeat
and re-live the clichés
of being in love, which
always feels new and
as if for the first time.

It all feels right again
for the time it will last,
made new, making
life more difficult,
but living easier.

Role Models

Autumn begins with a mellow Indian
summer day. Leaves only just lighten
into yellows, no wind to ruffle
the sun's even long rays warming
the soil for one last afternoon.

Big little strong boy with his
knife at the ready stakes out
the avenue, hiding in gardens,
waiting for weaklings behind trees,
clutching the day's proceeds.

Little old lady seems to shuffle
along through the first fallen leaves,
not looking where she is going,
not caring, her mind on other
things, the autumn sun perhaps.

A quick glance round and
then he pounces. She turns
and shocks him slightly; for
she is not afraid. He pulls
the knife on her, and—

that was his big mistake:
she calmly grasps his arm,
twists it a little and pulls,
then kicks his legs from under
him. His fall follows the knife's.

She pockets the knife and his
day's income, gives him a
final kick, already absent-
mindedly and then walks
on, her mind on autumn days.

Exotic and Other Flowers

'In deepest friendship' he'd written
inside the book he sent me after
some weeks, yet we had only known

each other for three days; short days
and brief encounters: yes, I too like the
theatre and teaching has many rewards.

Large head, grey hair, red beard: Abraham
may have looked like this. We talked and
touched and smiled a lot, growing

more congenial and closer on each
occasion. I like you. I've missed you.
Watching the town become familiar: our

sights, our pubs, our meals together and
with others. One touch too many and the
fire was kindled: his face had changed:

Greek god perhaps, or satyr, but I did
not yet know him well. I never
did. There was no time. He had to catch

a train and plane and I to write a lecture.
Today I remembered his inscription when
I went to the women's house, needing

help with the names of exotic flowers.
They seemed to have known me for years:
while eating, talking, cooking, reading

and planning their day, they showered
me with jasmine, magnolia and bougain-
villaea, with lilac, roses and sweet pea;

thistles, carnations and freesias; anemones,
tulips and violets, peonies, dandelion and
polyanthus; baskets of exotic exuberance.

Evzen Rattay Playing Elaine Agnew's 'Philip's Peace'

He sits as if embraced
by stronger forces than his own.
He and his cello breathe as one.
Their waves of sound wash and renew
the air and offer Philip peace.

A Perfect Still Life

The stone and the pearl
make a perfect still life,
so still you can only
sense the grinding of tears.

Honey and Seville Oranges

It hadn't been you who'd complained,
but your sisters had made you.
Childhood rivalry revisited:
your pride, their envy, jealousy,
too, in the illusion that motherhood
was mostly honey, when lemons
and Seville oranges were equal parts.

You sometimes forgot with the distance
that being close did not require
proximity, but you often remembered.
You'd much value a visit, my brother
had said, and I came from afar,
but as usual we could not bear
each other's presence for more than a week.

It hadn't been you who'd complained,
but your sisters: getting their own
back: 'children's duty', and wanting
a visit, too, a pleasant, brief and
sunny one. They inflated your desire
to see me, and once again I left
feeling deflated, guilty and sad.

Seashore Communication

Drawn to the source of life,
but watching the ocean's waves
going about their usual business:
healing, destroying, bleaching.

Flotsam carried ashore to join
the driftwood and half
a clean, white ribcage
of a presumably not prehistoric
cow: agriculture on the beach.

A long way from the deep of
the sea: culture came later,
recycling hope in ever new guises
as nature recycles itself.

Mistress sea, ruler of the foreshore,
drawn away only by the moon,
when life emerges from beneath
the desert of dead shells and washed
stones, and among them the keyboard

and one leg of a stranded piano,
battered by wind and water: craft,
communication, art: left dry,
if not too high for other references:

a rope, still tarry in places,
but it seems to have travelled
the earth a few times, disregarding
plumb lines, compasses or sextants,
curled round a piece of bottle-glass.

Art and knowledge feed
on nature and nature feeds
on itself: fishbone, bird's
wing and a dead piano.

Play It Again

Swifts darting from underneath the crown
of the big beech, gliding over the fields,
getting their feed open-mouthed, to and fro,
danger to insects, image of freedom.

Now I stir as I watch them, when I
think of the years of false trust and lying;
the usual sting: the eyes always had
it—this time they are brown, of the deep, dark
chocolate variety: at one glance

the Casablanca syndrome: still lurking,
half-forgotten. His malt, my red wine, heat;
being strangers, strange together in a
strange place: possibly war and resistance,
certainly adventure and romantic
illusion: claustrophobic and cloying,

freedom, liberation; also perhaps
primeval: the urge to couple before
the doom, translated into undying
passion, unfulfillable love. Shadows
falling between meeting and matching. But
play it again—for the memory, and
the darting swifts, the softly falling rain.

Not Kennedy's But Stalin's Death

Yes, I do remember when JFK was shot,
if vaguely; I can't be certain that I owned
a radio then, but I'm sure I heard it that day,
somewhere in the halls, stairs or showers of that
student house. My first year of real independence,
away from home; and what really mattered was my
diet, the next assignment to be wrung from
the library, and how to turn my crush into
a boyfriend. The Cold War had begun to thaw, I dimly
remember, and my father was two years dead.

Ten years before in a small kitchen, the only
properly heated room in a small house, we sat
by the radio listening and waiting for reports
from Moscow. It was cold outside, but I have
forgotten whether there was snow still on the ground.
My father intense—I can't recall what he said
when the final news came, but it does not matter.
There was a great sense of relief and possibly
new hope. My father, lame since childhood, walking
always with a stick, had always insisted
that given a chance, he'd go back home, even on
foot and backwards. That hope must have died over
the years. No one changed history to give him that chance.

Kythera

Kapsali

He's just turned forty
and looks as handsome
as ever: tall, fit,
a reddish beard and
now thinning blond hair,
tanned and healthy on
the beach. But I hadn't
realised that growing
older affected
my brother: he frets
about the onset
of a belly which
I cannot see and
feels not as fit and
young as before. I
had assumed that for
him, too, age would not
matter. His and his
wife's lives had lit up
with the birth and growth
of their son, just three
now and a delight.
So why should he mourn
the loss of his youth,
the slight hardening
of his muscles; what
has poisoned his mind?

Camping

They keep the campers caged,
from where they watch, grasping
the wire of the fence,
the day awakening

45

over the harbour, or
this morning's event: a
helicopter landing
after searching in vain
all night for the swimmer
lost since last afternoon.

The accident

Woken, very early, in
the narrow bed of this rented
sunny room, by a sound which
feels like home, only louder,
more threatening, as if to
engulf me: just outside my
window a helicopter
has landed. Everyone
out on their balconies: what
has happened, what's going
on? Rumours at first: a boat
lost in last night's storm. Was there
a storm? All was calm. Slowly
a story emerges: two
people swimming through the straits
between this and a tiny
island, one giving up half
way there, the other went on
and didn't make it. The coast
guard alerted at two in
the morning had searched
all night, but without success.
Next day his wife is quoted
to have said that he had been
a strong swimmer all his life.
They find the body a few
days later and every time
we swim we think of him and
all those the sea has engulfed.

On the beach

I could not find the watery
silver sickle of the very
new moon, just on the edge between
the dusty grey-blue of the sea's
horizon and the deep blue of
the sky which you pointed out to
me again and again with your
arm and hand and then even with
a water bottle as a marker.
I stared and stared, but did not see;
but then, I did not know either
why I was so aggressive, as
we sat on the beach, in response
to almost every word you said.

Do not disturb my circles, old
Pythagoras said before he
died. That I quite understand; it
was on another sandy beach.

Evening drive

Leaving the Peloponnese:—after
the garish lights of the isthmus and
Loutraki have faded there is a
stretch of land where the stars of the sky
meet the street lighting as a human
continuation, melting into
each other indistinguishably.
I understand why here one could be
optimistic about the future—
until, further down the road towards
Athens, the oil refineries' sky-
line generates its own firmament.

Morning

Waking in Athens after two weeks on
a windy island, the morning traffic
sounds like the wind against the walls and
windows as you wait for the waves' lapping.

The caves of Koutouki

Leaving behind central Athens' cats, pigeons
and cockroaches we climb to the caves above:
lit to show just enough of their mysteries,
slippery passages through glistening rock,
from cave to cave, damp and cool, oppressive in
their endless past; the murmur of the tourists, awed
by the ancient strata, giggling sometimes; guides
revealing the faces in the stone, their myths
and stories read into the rock formations.

Almost everywhere huge stalactites drip down
meeting stalagmites building up: they are said
to grow ten centimetres in a hundred
years. Eerily a whisper loudly echoes
through the cave: 'the language of philosophy
is a male act'. For millions of years these caves
have grown, predating the pre-Socratics, and
not counting on humankind's late arrival.

A Homecoming

I went straight east that mid-autumn and stopped
just south of the Baltic. There was dirty wet snow
on the streets of Warsaw and too much grey in the breeze-
blocks and concrete until we drove to Chopin's home
and visited some artists in the country: flat earth
and willows, poplars and birches. Pyramid and
poppy-seed cakes, strong coffee wafting through well-
heated houses; mild pickles: lots of dill and onion,
some sugar, little garlic; liqueurs and liquor ... for
the adults; and people were friendly, or polite, or
blunt, how they moved, how they ate and encouraged
us to eat and drink ... It was good to recover what
had become almost submerged in the western
regions of my living. I must come back for other seasons.

Eternity in Taganrog
found poem

The eternal flame burning
in the Russian city of Taganrog
to honour those killed
in the Second World War
went out after the city
failed to pay its gas bill.

Flirt

We shared the headache pills
that made you dizzy and
caused my sleeplessness:
you are the night owl,
the sleeplessness, the image
floating through my dreams,
gently lean, diving, rolling
through light night air
or fresh green waters,
stretching, hiding a steely core.

The tricks it plays
with sly smiles or
honest ones, sneaky
looks over the shoulder,
half-shy challenges,
recognising place and limits,
yet touching and feeling
for borders to be crossed;
the searching look
turning into laughter.

You touch my books
and offer me your knife
to cut my orange;
sometimes a strange,
streamlined swinging
together into dialogue
which seems to continue
the dream and feed
it again tonight.
Promises. Promises.

Chestnuts in May

We talk about the Lebanon,
at peace at last, resting,
embracing survival, happy,
but nervous about the future.

On University Road two people
embrace as if after a long time.

The chestnut trees are at their
best in May before their green and
joyous majesty is soiled by dust.

Northern Ireland News Dictionary

When do atrocities become atrocious?
Someone was killed. Again.
'... another atrocity has been committed
by the vile terrorists ... last night
another nefarious crime ...' Heinous,
cruel, wicked, vicious, perverted,
abominable. Repetition of condemnation
soon equals that of praise. Shortly
you'll be back to atrocious having
lost its meaning on the way.
It comes late in the old edition
of Roget's Thesaurus, under Class
Six: Affections, Section 4: Moral,
898 Malevolence and 934 Wickedness,
only followed by Section 5: Religion
where some of the last words are
ritual and credence.

Dublin-Perspective

Our problem in the North,
they say, but it isn't theirs
and it isn't a problem—
since there is no solution.
It's history
which sometimes
has outcomes.

Let Your Shadow

Let your shadow fall
over my shoulder, solid
and reassuring as a fruit
bursting open gently after
a full summer of ripening.
Let's dance while the old
rhythm remains and takes
the blood into our skin.
Let's stop tapping our
feet and spin a net
around us, forgetting
the question we never
needed to ask but
the outside begs, poses
and wants answered.
Let your shadow protect
us. Let it be our bed
and breakfast, our hello
and goodbye. Let your
shadow stay, when you leave.

The Site of Railway Tracks in Co. Sligo

Only the map's imagination sees
tracks of the railway branch line between Kilfree
Junction and Ballaghaderreen, where fences,
brambles and nettles bar my way; there is
nothing left but the site of what once connected
people and enticed further afield.

Then there were cattle trains on tracks criss-crossing
Europe, Jews being travelled one way, a little
later refugees took the opposite route,
and most of *us* survived the journey.

And finally the English couple, holding
up the queue at the luggage x-ray machine
in Vienna's airport lounge, moved on, feeling

hustled and frail: 'He said the knife was pointed.
Of course it was pointed', and he replied
'I suppose once they get suspicious they
look at everything, which isn't fair, really.'

Mahlberg, April 1995

Most trees are still undressed, though some begin
to sheath themselves in veils of merest
misty green, so light it's almost yellow.

Pit is fifty, a baby survivor
of a war which grabbed his father early,
long after it was lost. Only now does
he begin to look less like Papi, but

my memory is vague, perhaps resisting:
That summer, thirty-five years ago, he
wrote letters twice a week to his wayward
daughter: Pit made a good kitchen maid and
even Buschi peeled potatoes, while Mutti

was away recovering from exhaustion
in a Schwarzwald Home. A year later he
was dead; the last photos on the film I
brought from Mexico—the camera lent
by the geography teacher—were the last
ones of him: serene, gentle, the irony

almost gone from his face, almost healthy,
perhaps even happy. How I hated
his biting irony which drew fear from
me every time. There was none of it in
those letters; they kept me informed about
the fate of the hamster and how the household
ticked over without the women in the house,

while I encountered the world, the big
adventure. And he had helped, from a small
purse, and despite his stern parenting:
punctuality, responsibility,
hard work, and accountability. Every
mark counted, and I'd miss two weeks of

school, a major offence, and never caught
up with, yet I went crazy in my
vulnerability over Leni's
cut daffodils which I did not want to die.
At night the marten leaves dirt-marks on the

glass roof of the veranda, shy, sly, owing
obedience only to the moon. I did
not know my father as an adult, I
accepted that he thought me not an equal

at eighteen, and resented it, but I
loved him, of course, unconditional at
first, and then with reservations. There was

no time to prove myself to him, nor am
I sure he wanted that or could have coped.

Visiting Mutti

Once a year I come, sitting with you
for ten days or so, trying to communicate.
It's not as if your mind is gone, even

though your sight is, and your bones are always
near breaking point. The telly had to be
on loudly all the time, but now that it's

broken you insist that you never wanted
anything but the radio. Talking through
that is equally difficult, and you

resist all our suggested tapes. Our
conversation is minimal: I can't
get through to you. Or so I think: you love

the flowers I brought, but reject the fruit
as inappropriate; nothing much seems
to interest you any more. Yet your

head used to be full of stories and
memories and I'm sure it still is,
you just can't be bothered any more.

I feel so utterly helpless, trying
to make you talk, trying to make you
remember at least; you just like me

to be there.—As a child, dependent,
but remembering that you were once
in control; now the child seems to know

what's best for you most of the time. No wonder
you rebel, but recalcitrant as
a child who loves and hates equally, helplessly.

Portrait of a Woman

Her hands caress the vase
she once brought from the Levant,
the cushions and hangings; she waters
the plants in their pots.

As the rain drips and drips,
softly but relentlessly,
she closes the door, and then
the windows with great firmness,

to keep out whatever might
want to come in. It's not just
the weather: she used to love walking
in the rain, defying it, joining it.

Her dress is scarlet with brown
and olive stripes, her greying hair
is held by a scarf of sheerest silk,
the leather belt makes her feel straight.

But something broke: she wanted
to conquer life, now it frightens her;
she used to have passions,
now she's reduced to anxieties.

She won't open the windows again
until the sun returns, she never
travels much these days, her only
adventures are the books she writes.

A Wet July in Co. Sligo

In hot climates I never
want to think of the cool North-
West again. Not for me
the consoling soft rain and
the bracing winds from the Atlantic,
where roses often bloom all
year and temperatures rarely
fall below the needs of growing grass.

I love the sun when it burns
down from an even blue sky.
Its softer northern version may
be more welcome, but I'd rather
suffer its stings and its sweat,
and wallow in its indulgence
which does away with the need
to dress and makes me feel whole.

Yet it's in the North-West that I've
made my life, where people draw
the curtains when the sun comes out
to save the carpets. It makes
me yearn for the sun's healing
power, its consoling harshness
bracing me against boredom.

Anna's Visit

There's a strange mixture of this
quiet landscape and then
suddenly all this violence from
elsewhere in your poems, she said.

Full of apprehension she went
to visit Belfast for a day
expecting tension and rudeness.
Up the Falls and back by bus,

up the Shankhill and back on
the Crumlin Road. How friendly
all the people are, how helpful;
it feels like a good place, a

welcoming place to live in.
It is, Anna, it is a
peaceful, friendly place, with violence
woven into its texture.

The Strausses

Johann's waltzes,
not like a polka's
earthy touch but all
movement and glitter,
and touching only
for gravity's sake,
since the movement
of two together
is even lighter and
more exhilarating
than your own.

Richard's music
delves deep into
less chartered waters,
sentimental sometimes,
but always searching
for the depth of
depression and
the peak of elation.
They moved Vienna
and Munich
at different times.

A September

The summer is exhausted.
Only in the tidiest
gardens are there no dead
flower-heads among the bloom.

The summer wants to finish
with fruit and seed and be
done with; but all this
deadheading forces more

and more flowering, in all
the front gardens as in front
of Kensington Palace.
With all the emotions

and colours still in full flow
the summer looks drained; it wants
to heed its exhaustion,
call a halt and rest.

Graham's Boxes
for Graham Gingles

As a young artist he sliced
maggots and stuffed flies to get
to the heart of the matter:

and now his interiors,
intricate and delicate,
are well furnished with hearts, bones,

bowels and intestines; flags,
mindsets and dreams enacted
in miniature, crafted in

wood or plastic, colourful
or bleached to essentials, womb
and vulva, skeletal

hands, pelvis and backbone, an
eerie glance from a passing
face, pinned down, nicely encased

and encapsulated, a
Peeping Tom's view of human
construct and composition.

R.E.M.

You blink and it's gone:
the present is the moment
when the future
becomes the past.

The fear and freedom of dreaming,
unrestrained by material bonds,
digesting reality, building experience,
the brain's nightly sorting and filing.

Deprived of dreams, messages can't
be delivered, transmission is
retarded, facts pile up, not
knowing where to go and what
they are or what they're for.

It begins to fester; its aroma
will be a wound under your
fingernails and creep into your
skin until even a nightmare
would be a relief.

The loss of dreams
is the loss of time:
present cannot
become past,
future cannot
unfold.

Agadir

From the window

Hibiscus, agaves, cacti, bougainvillaea,
oleander, argen trees; roses, too, and
honeysuckle; prickly pears beyond picking;
almonds and Seville oranges almost ripe.

Muezzin

The muezzin's early morning call almost
drowns the traffic noise as the mist rolls in from
the Atlantic, and the shops open ready
to sell spirits, and not just to tourists, while
Mohammed's hand melts in my handshake.

Tuareg

With the women back home in the tents of the
Sahara creating the carpets he sells,
he tries it on with the tourists: come with me
on my camel in the desert, marry me,
and we'll sleep on these carpets under the moon
in the peace of the sand. I could have been his
mother and had only bought an old silver
ring, yet I wonder how often he succeeds.

Marrakesh

It is transparent why the hippies loved it:
intoxicating, enchanting, casting its
spell of perfumed spices, lucky charms; dark souks
ablaze with colour—after the hippies came
the package tourists, and clever traders have
learned to assess their visitors at a glance,
on their background and degree of wealth, laying

down potential custom and mercilessly
chase them until the tourist police catches
on and intervenes. But late into the night
you succumb to the lights, smells, sounds and colours.

Stars

Caroline said, she'd rarely seen so few
stars, but it must have been the tourist lights of
Agadir suppressing their shining, forcing
them into the shadow. I've rarely seen so
many, so brilliant and large as on the night-
road from Marrakesh, joining the Milky Way.

Moving in Suburbia

The improvement is that the sounds
from next door at night are just
semi-detached tones of soothing
excitement, through a wall gently,
not earth-shattering, nor quite sound-
proof; proximity cushioned, if
still maintained as the hedges, low
or high, dividing the gardens,

where self-righteousness blooms in all
of us, easily hurt, smelling
the barbecue, putting a foot
down where we shouldn't, defenceless;
so vulnerable we sometimes
believe nothing will ever hurt
us again: unprotected we
compete even for the greatest
sensitivity, open wounds
all over, slowly scarring with
the years' rotting garden clippings.

But at first the lawny expanse
lulls you into believing that
here at last you'll hold your own and,
with neighbours you do and don't know,
cup your hands round your pain, relax
until soon they'll move or you do.

Making Hay

The wind ripples the grass which
is growing longer now. Do
they make hay here, asks Seymour,
and unthinkingly I say
yes, sometimes, but it is more
likely to be silage than
hay they make, thanks to the rain
and the lack of sunshine. And
I look at the photo once
more: the first time I look old.

No More Cinderellas

Cinderella has to leave at midnight,
he said, but I stayed; for my prince has come,
not as he imagines, but shaped out of
the aspirations raked from the ashes
to make my own shoes, my own carriage and
horses, my own house. Transforming rescue
is no longer necessary, thank you.

Snow Queen

My limbs are the Queen of Snow,
as you observed before: right
to the bone of a cooling heart,
all my colours turned inward
and my skin grows pale as rain.

For me Jerusalem holds secrets,
where tissue hasn't been softened
for years. Now that the days grow
longer and soon the sun will warm
again, I know where the line is.

For you the world is child's play.
Where does it run? The child's difficult
task: I raked the lawn today and
the sun touched my face to excitement,
my body expecting to tan again.

Do you hold the City in false trust?
the Four Gated, the Golden One
of which I dream and its treasures
gleam as sea-glitter running from
oppressive voices seductively.

Greetings

He greeted me
the French way
and turned
the other cheek.
Better than words
which can kill
more efficiently,
and better than
a cold shoulder.